P9-BJG-269

Off the Page

Ron Benson

Lynn Bryan

Kim Newlove

Charolette Player

Liz Stenson

CONSULTANTS

Susan Elliott

Diane Lomond

Ken MacInnis

Elizabeth Parchment

LIBRARY
Meridian Heights School

Prentice Hall Ginn Canada
Scarborough, Ontario

Contents

Bibliography

 Selections with this symbol are available on audio.

 This symbol indicates student writing.

🍁 Canadian selections are marked with this symbol.

HOW MUSIC WAS FETCHED OUT OF HEAVEN

retold by Geraldine McCaughrean
Illustrated by Hélène Bouliane

Once the world suffered in Silence. Not that it was a quiet place, nor peaceful, for there was always the groan of the wind, the crash of the sea, the grumble of lava in the throats of volcanoes, and the grate of a man's ploughshare through the stony ground. Babies could be heard crying at night, and women in the daytime, because of the hardness of life and the great unfriendliness of Silence.

Tezcatlipoca, his body heavy as clay and his heart heavy as lead (for he was the Lord of Matter), spoke to Quetzalcoatl, feathery Lord of Spirit. He spoke from out of the four quarters of the Earth, from the north, south, easterly, and westerly depths of the iron-hard ground. "The world needs music, Quetzalcoatl! In the thorny glades and on the bald seashore, in the square comfortless houses of the poor and in the dreams of the sleeping, there should be music, there ought to be song. Go to Heaven, Quetzalcoatl, and fetch it down!"

"How would I get there? Heaven is higher than wings will carry me."

"String a bridge out of cables of wind, and nail it with stars: a bridge to the Sun. At the feet of the Sun, sitting on the steps of his throne, you will find four musicians. Fetch them down here. For I am so sad in this Silence, and the People are sad, hearing the sound of Nothingness ringing in their ears."

"I will do as you say," said Quetzalcoatl, preening his green feathers in readiness for the journey. "But will they come, I ask myself. Will the musicians of the Sun want to come?"

He whistled up the winds like hounds. Like hounds they came bounding over the bending treetops, over the red places where dust rose up in twisting columns, and over the sea, whipping the waters into mountainous waves. Baying and howling, they carried Quetzalcoatl higher and higher—higher than all Creation—so high that he could glimpse the Sun ahead of him. Then the four mightiest winds plaited themselves into a cable, and the cable swung out across the void of Heaven: a bridge planked with cloud and nailed with stars.

"Look out, here comes Quetzalcoatl," said the Sun, glowering, lowering, his red-rimmed eyes livid. Circling him in a cheerful dance, four musicians played and sang. One, dressed in white and shaking bells, was singing lullabies; one, dressed in red, was singing songs of war and passion as he beat on a drum; one, in sky-blue robes fleecy with cloud, sang the ballads of Heaven, the stories of the gods; one, in yellow, played on a golden flute.

This place was too hot for tears, too bright for shadows. In fact the shadows had all fled downwards and clung fast to people. And yet all this sweet music had not served to make the Sun generous. "If you don't want to have to leave here and go down where it's dark, dank, dreary, and dangerous, keep silent, my dears. Keep silent, keep secret, and don't answer when Quetzalcoatl calls," he warned his musicians.

Across the bridge rang Quetzalcoatl's voice. "O singers! O marvellous makers of music. Come to me. The Lord of the World is calling!" The voice of Quetzalcoatl was masterful and inviting, but the Sun had made the musicians afraid. They kept silent, crouching low, pretending not to hear. Again and again Quetzalcoatl called them, but still they did not stir, and the Sun smiled smugly and thrummed his fingers on the sunny spokes of his chairback. He did not intend to give up his musicians, no matter who needed them.

So Quetzalcoatl withdrew to the rain-fringed horizon and, harnessing his four winds to the black thunder, had them drag the clouds closer, circling the Sun's citadel. When he triggered the lightning and loosed the thunderclaps, the noise was monumental. The Sun thought he was under siege.

Thunder clashed against the Sun with the noise of a great brass cymbal, and the musicians, their hands over their ears, ran this way and that looking for help. "Come out to me, little makers of miracles," said Quetzalcoatl in a loud but gentle voice. *BANG* went the thunder, and all Heaven shook.

The crooner of lullabies fluttered down like a sheet blown from a bed. The singer of battle songs spilled himself like blood along the floor of Heaven and covered his head with his arms. The singer of ballads, in his fright, quite forgot his histories of Heaven, and the flutist dropped his golden flute. Quetzalcoatl caught it.

As the musicians leapt from their fiery nest, he opened his arms and welcomed them into his embrace, stroking their heads in his lap. "Save us, Lord of Creation! The Sun is under siege!"

"Come, dear friends. Come where you are needed most."

The Sun shook and trembled with rage like a struck gong, but he knew he had been defeated, had lost his musicians to Quetzalcoatl.

At first the musicians were dismayed by the sadness and silence of the Earth. But no sooner did they begin to play than the babies in their cribs stopped squalling. Pregnant women laid a hand on their big stomachs and sighed with contentment. The laborers in

the fields cupped their hands to their ears and shook themselves, so that their shadows of sadness fell away in the noonday. Children started to hum. Young men and women got up to dance, and in dancing fell in love. Even the mourner at the graveside, hearing sweet flute music, stopped crying.

Quetzalcoatl himself swayed his snaky hips and lifted his hands in dance at the gate of Tezcatlipoca, and Tezcatlipoca came out of doors. Matter and Spirit whirled together in a dance so fast: had you been there, you would have thought you were seeing only one.

And suddenly every bird in the sky opened its beak and sang, and the stream moved by with a musical ripple. The sleeping child dreamed music and woke up singing. From that day onwards, life was all music—rhythms and refrains, falling cadences and fluting calls. No one saw just where the Sun's musicians settled or made their homes, but their footprints were everywhere and their bright colors were found in corners that had previously been grey and cobwebbed with silence. The flowers turned up bright faces of red and yellow and white and blue, as if they could hear singing. Even the winds ceased to howl and roar and groan, and learned love songs.

ABOUT THE AUTHOR — GERALDINE McCAUGHREAN

Born and educated in North London, England, Geraldine McCaughrean studied to become a teacher, but she never taught. Instead, after she graduated she worked on children's books at a London publishing company. She then went on to become the award-winning author of several novels and a radio play. Several of her books include retellings of tales from myths to Shakespeare. Geraldine says, ". . . I can't get enough of reading and retelling them [myths and legends]: it's more fun than anything." Geraldine currently lives in Berkshire, England, with her husband and daughter.

Creators

Illustrated by Leon Zernitski

I am the creativity

by Alexis De Veaux

I am the dance step
of the paintbrush singing
I am the sculpture
of the song
the flame breath
of words
giving new life to paper
yes, I am the creativity
that never dies
I am the creativity
keeping my people
alive

The Artist

by Ashley Bryan

I know a man
Like a child
He loves to paint
He can paint anything
He sets his heart to

He knows
That to have
Anything he loves
He can have it
Fair and forever
If he paints
A picture of it

He knows
That to face
Anything that hurts
He can do it
Transform the sorrow
If he paints
A picture of it

This is how he lives
This is what he does

A Young Painter
The Life and Paintings of Wang Yani

by Zheng Zhensun and Alice Low

Wang Yani is a young Chinese artist who paints in the centuries-old tradition of Chinese brush painting. She grew up in the small town of Gongcheng in southern China, and is largely self-taught. Today she has painted more than ten thousand paintings and has held solo exhibitions of her art in Japan, Hong Kong, Germany, the United States, and Great Britain.

Wang Yani painting in the Confucian temple in Gongcheng.

How Yani Paints

Like many other people, Yani started to draw by doodling dots and lines. But in less than a year, she passed that stage of early childhood drawing, a stage that most children take years to get through. Yani also mastered the art of using brush and ink when she was a very young child. At the age of three, while other children could barely draw recognizable figures, she was painting her pictures of lively cats and monkeys.

Yani's paintings are fresh, vigorous, and bold. A Japanese artist, Yikuo Hiyayama, commented on the works Yani painted at this early age. He said they were "solid in structure, with smooth brushwork, and clear lines." He said they did not have any unnecessary polishing, for Yani had known just what to omit, and he also stated that she knew how to use the paper in a way that would bring out its ability to soak up paint.

Yani holds her brush in different ways according to the size of the brush and the way she thinks is best for her. Once, when Yani's schoolteacher wanted her to hold the brush in a way that was unnatural to her, Yani's father interfered. He encouraged Yani to go back to holding the brush in her own way.

Yani's father has also advised her never to fix her eyes on the tip of the brush as she paints, but to scan the whole sheet of paper and even beyond it so as to have a wide field of vision. As time has gone by, Yani's brushstrokes have become more powerful. Now, with a few rapid sweeps of the brush and a soft twist of her wrist, Yani swiftly paints an old green tree and adds a tail to a monkey.

Yani handles the brush with ease, sometimes painting swiftly, sometimes slowly, sometimes cleverly, sometimes bluntly, and sometimes unevenly. She also uses ink in different ways—dry, moist, strong, and light—to create different effects.

When Yani was very young, she could not concentrate on her painting as deeply as she does now. She used to leave her painting to play after doing only a few

I Want Fruit
Age 3
33 cm x 66 cm

brushstrokes. Sometimes while painting she sang, danced, chatted, made faces, and even imitated other people and animals.

Now that Yani is older, she approaches her painting a little differently. Before she paints, she calms herself to clear her mind and then waits for inspiration. But when she starts painting, she does not know exactly what she will paint. The idea develops as she works. Yani likes to listen to music on her Walkman while she paints. She believes that music stimulates her feelings. Her favorite music is Chinese music, Beethoven's Fifth Symphony, and works by Schubert and Mozart.

Yani's father never comments on his daughter's work in her presence, for he doesn't want her to paint according to *his* likes and dislikes. Nor does he expect her to do perfect work. In his opinion, if he were to consider her work to be perfect, her imaginative ideas would probably dry up. He wants Yani, the child artist, to keep searching for ways to push her experience and knowledge forward.

Yani never does any copying, nor does she paint from life. She remembers everything she sees, and she paints her lively pictures completely from memory. One example of her amazing visual memory occurred when, as a young child, Yani asked her father to write some words for her to copy. Yani's father did not want her to copy his way of writing Chinese characters, so he wrote them in the air with his fingers. Yani watched his movements very carefully and proceeded to write the characters on paper, just as her father had drawn them.

Yani's father encourages Yani to remember what she has seen during the day and to paint what has affected her the most. He has always stressed that Yani should paint her impressions of the things she has seen, rather than concentrating on the details and special features. That is why there are no peaks in Yani's paintings of beautiful Guilin. Instead, she has painted her overall impressions that the Guilin landscape has left in her mind.

Likewise, though Yani's monkeys are very lively and have all the traits of these mischievous animals, none of them is painted true to form. They are the products of her impressions after her many trips to the zoo. Some of their gestures are simply from Yani's imagination. Instead of reproducing their actual behavior, Yani let her monkeys reflect her own feelings about them.

Her first monkeys were without hair or toes, but her father did not point this out to her because he knew that his small daughter had to pass through a certain process before becoming familiar with her subject. He knew that Yani would make changes in the way she painted the monkeys within the natural course of time. Though Yani did give her monkeys hair and toes as she grew older, her monkeys were still not painted in great detail. They were Yani's overall impression of monkeys.

When Yani was eight years old, her father made a painful personal decision in order to further protect his daughter's originality and creativity. He quit painting altogether, even though he was rising to the peak of his career. His oil paintings were shown at every art exhibition in Guangxi, and the largest one, *Liberate Guangxi,* was in the collection of the regional museum.

Why did he cut short his painting career? The reason was that he was afraid his style of painting, using oils rather than Chinese brush and ink, would have a poor effect on Yani, who painted with traditional Chinese materials and used many of the traditional Chinese brushstrokes.

Wang Shiqiang's friends have asked him if he feels sad about giving up his oil painting.

"Yes," he said, "but I see in Yani a more promising artist than Wang Shiqiang. I have a duty to help and protect her so that she will use her artistic talents fully." He added that he hopes to go back to his own painting when Yani turns eighteen.

Mountain in Spring
Age 8
30 cm x 33 cm

The Ripe Fruit
Age 12
33 cm x 135 cm

Yani and Her Father

Though Wang Shiqiang has protected Yani's creativity and freedom to express herself, he has also furnished her with guidance and stimulation, and he has done everything possible to create an atmosphere that would lead to her artistic growth.

Not only did he introduce her to the beauties of nature while she was very young, but he also took her to interesting places, which stimulated her mind.

After Yani was four, she went with her father to many cities where her work was exhibited, and so she had many wonderful experiences. She climbed the Taishan Mountains and the Great Wall, visited the Palace Museum in Beijing and the Confucian temple in Qufu, Shandong Province. In recent years she has toured many countries, and these trips have expanded her knowledge and broadened her artistic approach.

And though Yani's father has been cautious about giving advice to Yani, he has helped to strengthen her understanding of the things she has seen.

For instance, one day a botanist visited the Wang family, and Yani's father asked him to talk about the function of leaves, for Yani had painted trees without leaves. Yani listened to the botanist speak, and the next day, Yani's painting showed leaves on a tree. On the tip of each leaf hung a fruit. Yani also said, "Monkeys eat fruit, and fruit eat leaves." This was *her* understanding of the botanist's explanation of how leaves get their food. Though she could not absorb all of the facts, she was making progress. Soon after that, Wang Shiqiang took Yani to an orchard, where she saw that fruit grew on twigs.

Since then, Yani has painted many paintings of trees and fruit, and the fruit hangs from twigs, not from leaves!

Yani's father has helped her to see pictures in her mind by encouraging her to make up stories. When Yani was five, he took her to Guangzhou on a ship. Wang Shiqiang started telling Yani a story, then Yani responded with one of her own. To the astonishment of the passengers, the two of them told each other stories for seven hours!

Yani's father has also encouraged her to think independently and to solve problems by herself. In the Wangs' courtyard there is a hibiscus tree, which bears white flowers in the morning and red in the evening. Yani painted a picture and called it *Hibiscus Flowers Are White in the Morning*.

She painted the petals in a very light color and showed the painting to her father. "Doesn't this look beautiful?" she asked.

"Is this white?" asked Wang Shiqiang, for the petals looked quite grey.

Yani thought for a moment. Then she took her brush, dipped it in thick black ink, and painted the background dark. In contrast, the petals now looked white. Yani's father thought so, too, and nodded his head in approval.

Wang Shiqiang frequently created problems for Yani while she was painting, in order to sharpen her mind and make her more visually sensitive. One day, Yani drew a horizontal line across a sheet of paper. When her father asked her what she was going to paint, she answered, "A bridge."

"A bridge is not pleasing to the eye," said her father. "Why not paint something else?"

Yani thought for a few moments. Then quickly, she transformed the line into a shoulder pole with a basket of fruit hanging from either end. She added a little monkey carrying it and hurrying along.

Yani and her father have made it a rule that she should never say, "I don't know," when he asks her a question, for there is always an answer to be found.

"When Yani was painting, I would pretend not to know anything about what she was after," said Wang Shiqiang. "Every time she would finish a painting, I would ask her why it was painted in that certain way; for example, why there was so much space left in the painting. Yani would never say, 'I don't know.' Instead, she would think about what I had asked." He added that if their views differed because of the difference in their ages, he would just say, "I don't necessarily agree with you." Sometimes, when Yani's painting didn't seem to make sense to him, he would praise her on purpose and even say, "It's wonderful." Then Yani would keep on painting enthusiastically, until she herself realized what a mess she had made.

When Yani's father treated her this way, his aim was to build up her thinking and creativity, rather than to let her mind drift. "Inspiration and guidance, when given in an appropriate way, are essential to protect and develop a child's ability to imagine and create," he says. He adds that it is important to keep that guidance within the boundaries of the child's stage of development.

Yani's father loves her very much, but he can be strict with her when necessary. He feels that a good artist must have a strong character; therefore, discipline is important.

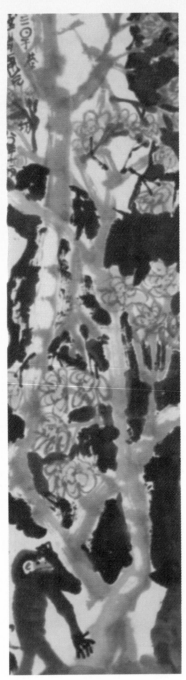

Hibiscus Flowers Are White in the Morning
Age 5
33 cm x 132 cm

Animals' Autumn
Age 14
97 cm x 179 cm

As Yani became famous, she became proud, too, and sometimes she lost her temper. Her father and his friends were concerned about this.

When Yani was four and a half years old, she put on a painting demonstration in the city of Yangzhou. Somebody overturned a cup by accident and wet the table on which she was working. She went into a rage, flung her brush away, and sat fuming, tight-lipped. Soon she started to paint again, but she did it half-heartedly.

Afterwards, Yani and her father returned to the hotel room, and her father told her that if she wanted to continue to be a painter she must be serious, not temperamental and arrogant.

Yani promised to paint seriously, saying, "Papa, I love painting. I want to paint." But her father insisted that she stop. Yani broke into tears and told her father that more than anything she wanted to keep on painting. Just then, he was called out of the room.

When her father returned with a friend, he was surprised to see that the whole floor was covered with Yani's paintings, each done in all seriousness. Yani looked up with tears in her eyes and said, "I can never paint again. These are my last works."

Her father said, "You have already apologized by words. And the paintings on the floor show you realize the mistake you have made." He told Yani that now she could continue to paint.

Wang Shiqiang's friend said to him, "You are really too strict with your daughter. But you are right. We must be strict with child prodigies who have won a name for themselves."

In 1985, when Yani was ten years old, she was interviewed by some sixty reporters in a big Tokyo hotel. One reporter asked, "We in Japan regard you as a great talent. How do you feel about that?"

"I feel nothing special," answered Yani, amid the flashes and clicks of cameras.

"Are your paintings the best in the world?"

"No," answered Yani. "If mine are, what about the works of other famous artists?"

Carving a Totem Pole

*Written and photographed
by Vickie Jensen*

Before our history was ever written down, the old people kept all the knowledge in their heads. They were the only "books" that there were. They used totem poles to teach us about the past. It was important to them that the children know their ancestors at an early age because they, too, would become the history books of our people.

The elders would take children aside and tell them a story. The next day they'd tell it to them again. The elders told their legends over and over. When I was a child I used to sit with my uncle and listen to his stories. This is the way that I learned about my family history.

I want children to understand the importance of the totem pole. I want them to know that poles helped our people to learn our family history for generations and generations, all the way back to mythical times.

When a totem pole is raised up, it is like a birth of an important person. The pole is given a name and treated with the same kind of respect you would give a chief. Like the elders, each pole is a teacher, a storyteller.

*Norman Tait
Nisg̱a'a Artist*

In the past, there were many different kinds of totem poles. Some were carved in memory of a chief's death. Others supported the massive beams of a house. Some held the remains of a dead chief or were grave markers. A few were giant figures set up at the beach to welcome visitors. Male and female chiefs had poles made that told the mythic stories of their families. The characters of these stories were carved onto the pole, including the family's crests, or spiritual ancestors. Today some totem poles are carved for museums, shopping malls, businesses, or education centres. None of them have family stories or crests, so Norman Tait has chosen a story of his own to use on this pole.

Norman's design is based on a story about how people learned to live in harmony with the creatures of the sea, sky, and land. He has put Raven at the top of the pole, followed by Killerwhale, then Bear, and finally Man crouched over the doorway. He has also added a Moon figure between Raven's wings and has Bear holding a little Wolf cub. Around the doorway are four small human faces.

Working from drawings, Norman and Chip measure approximately how long each figure will be on the pole. Then Norman begins sketching Raven's face and wings, as well as the Moon figure. He draws freely, not worrying about where the exact lines will go. Later he pencils in darker, more definite, outlines.

Finally he prepares a full-size paper drawing of each of the remaining figures for other crew members to trace onto the wood. These tracings serve as guidelines and help Norman judge the exact size and placement of the figures.

Norman is impatient to begin cutting the first figures. He starts at the top of the pole, shaping Raven's forehead. Then, while crew members are still tracing the lower creatures, he begins shaping the legs of the Moon figure and Raven's wings. He alternates using his big adze, axe, and chain saw, seeing in his mind how deeply to cut. Chunks of wood fly off the pole. Norman calls these first cuts an explosion, and they feel like one!

There are two pieces of this totem pole that must be carved from separate blocks of wood and added on later— Whale's fin and Raven's beak. Norman gives the young apprentices the responsibility of carving these pieces. He assigns the beak to Isaac. Wayne will do the fin.

Norman, Chip, and Hammy rough cut the rest of the figures. Then Chip demonstrates how to use a mallet and chisel to define each creature from the background wood. At this point, all the arms, legs, and heads look square and chunky.

The next stage in carving the totem pole is rounding the figures and sculpting the faces. Isaac's strong adze strokes take the sharp edges off Bear's legs and arms. He is careful not to cut too deeply where Norman has drawn small circles on the wood. These mark the areas that will become the wrist bones and ankle bones that are a trademark of Norman's carving.

Chip puts his hands over the eyeballs, feeling whether or not they are equally shaped. The carvers learn how to measure with their hands as well as their eyes. "Your hands will tell you if one side is higher," he explains, "but you need to practise."

Each of the crew members will carve one of the four faces around the doorway all by himself. Norman calls these faces signature pieces, because they are a way of signing each carver's name to the totem pole. After the faces have been drawn on the wood, the carvers begin rough cutting with smaller, single-handed adzes. Although the faces are all drawn from the same outline, they soon look quite different from one another.

Working head to head, Hammy and Isaac use chisels and mallets to

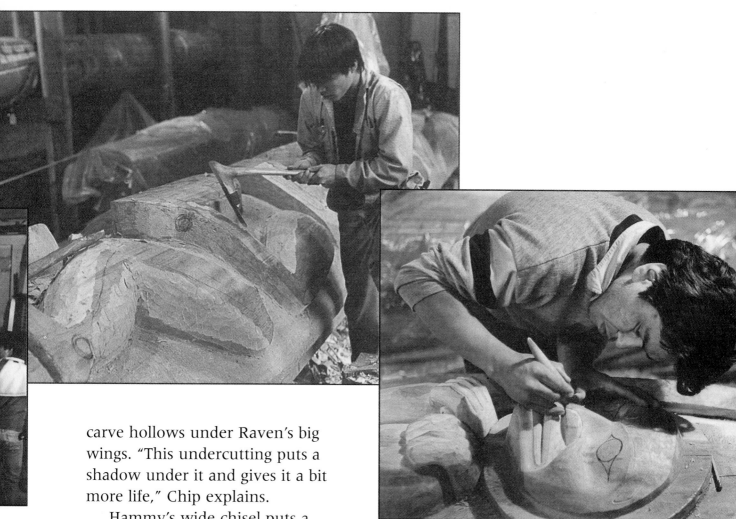

carve hollows under Raven's big wings. "This undercutting puts a shadow under it and gives it a bit more life," Chip explains.

Hammy's wide chisel puts a smooth finish on Man's legs. Carvers can also use a curved knife to make hundreds of tiny cuts that blend together for a textured finish. Sandpaper is never used on a totem pole.

Now the fin looks slim and streamlined. But Norman points out that the base of the fin is still too thick. It needs to be cut down more. He wants it to flow naturally out of the body of the whale. When the fin and beak are completely finished, they will be attached to the pole with waterproof glue and wooden pins, called dowels.

On this pole, Norman's signature piece is baby Wolf. It represents his youngest son, Micah, who is Wolf clan. Norman is a high-ranking Eagle clan chief. But among the Nisg̱a'a, each child inherits his or her clan identity from the mother.

Nearly complete, this Wolf cub has chubby feet, curled hands, and an impish smile.

For finer work, the carvers switch to different tools. They use knives with straight-edged and curved blades that they have made themselves. Norman wants this totem pole to age naturally to a soft grey. So rather than paint it, crew members use their knives to cut V-shaped grooves around the eyes, eyebrows, and nostrils of each figure. These grooves, rather than color, highlight the figures.

Finally, after three months of learning and labor, the pole is done. "For us, carving a totem pole was just work, until we all stood back and looked at it," Chip explains. "Then everybody felt the same way. Wow, what a beautiful pole!"

It's time to move the completed pole to the Native Education Centre where it will be raised. The totem pole is as tall as eight people standing on each other's shoulders. And it is very heavy! Friends are invited to help carry the massive work of art. The crew members put on the ceremonial tunics and leggings that the family women have sewn for the pole raising. Norman wears his deerskin shirt and dance apron. He and Chip use drum signals to tell the carriers when to lift and how far to go.

Finally the totem pole is carefully loaded onto a long truck.

When the truck rolls up to the new building, the carvers and other family members welcome the pole with a Nisga'a song. Norman feels that a totem pole is a powerful storyteller and must be shown the same respect as a great chief.

The next day is the pole raising. Tait family members and other Nisga'a arrive early. All of them bring button blankets and other ceremonial items such as frontlets, rattles, and talking sticks. Although Norman's mind is full of details about the difficult pole raising, he still takes time to give his niece a reassuring hug.

Nowadays, some totem poles are quickly lifted into position using cranes. But Norman wants his pole raised in the traditional way. Hundreds of well-wishers, friends, and students from the Native Education Centre will pull up this totem pole by hand. They will use only ropes and pulleys, so it is important that the thick ropes be positioned properly.

Before the pole can be pulled upright, it must be carefully rolled over onto its side. Norman leaps up onto the pole. He drums out a signal to tighten the ropes and begin the turn.

Crowds of people pull on each of the lines. Slowly, slowly the pole inches skyward. The ropes creak and strain under the weight.

With a last push at the base, the massive totem pole finally slides into position. The crowd explodes with cheers and whistles. Grinning with joy, Hammy and Isaac hug each other.

Chip recalls, "When I looked up at the pole, I felt just like crying. I couldn't believe it!"

With the pole safely raised, the ceremonies begin. Norman puts on his button blanket and a finely carved eagle helmet. He drums as his mother sings a welcoming song for the pole. Finally, clutching a handful of eagle feathers, Norman dances.

The members of the crew stand proud in their regalia. Looking at them, Norman says, "I feel like I just brought up a whole family of kids, and now they're men."

Norman tells the story of the pole to the hundreds of people who have helped raise it. Then Wolf clan chief Mercy Robinson Thomas officially names the pole. She calls out the Nisga'a name, Wil Sayt Bakwhlgat, three times. The name means "the place where the people gather."

After speeches and a feast of deer meat stew, the crowd begins to leave. The carvers gather with their families at the base of the pole for photos. They want to remember this day always.

The director of the Native Education Centre explains that the building would have been cheaper to build without the pole. But then it would have looked like any other place. This totem pole says, "We're here! Native people are alive!"

ABOUT THE AUTHOR VICKIE JENSEN

Vickie Jensen enjoys a number of careers, including writing, teaching, and photography. Her interest in Northwest Coast Native culture began when she moved to British Columbia. Since then, Vickie and her husband have worked with elders to produce over thirty schoolbooks in a variety of Native languages. She has written two English-language books on the same subject: *Where the People Gather* and *Carving a Totem Pole*. Vicky has also written several maritime books, including *Saltwater Women at Work* and *Working These Waters*.

Wildland Visions
Newfoundland and Labrador

Written and photographed by Dennis Minty

Peace of Mind

I photograph what I love—the expanses and the details of this land that is my home. Their texture, color, moods, and interconnectedness are my inspiration. The wondrous light that bathes them shapes what I see. With camera in hand, I slow down, stop, and become absorbed by my surroundings. This process gives me peace of mind like nothing else. In fact that's what these pictures are—my peace of mind.

I owe this place, Newfoundland and Labrador, a great debt. It has given me a quality of life that I suspect is unattainable, for me, anywhere else on Earth. With these photographs, I pay tribute to my home.

On the Water

My supreme escape is to slip the mooring from my Twillingate-crafted, juniper-ribbed, fir-planked boat on a sunny summer day to poke in and out of the coves and between the islands of one of our radiant bays.

Each summer for the past decade my family has tented for a few weeks tucked in some out-of-the-way inlet. We bring all we need and devote ourselves to each other and the place in which we happen to be.

Bogs

Crammed with life, bogs are the tropical jungles of northern Canada. Out of curiosity, I once counted fifteen different plants in a tabloid-sized area of one of these great sopping sponges.

Impressed with their diversity and charm, for Christmas one year I even gave my mother a piece of bog transplanted into a large aluminum roaster. She watered it and nurtured it through the winter to be rewarded with lemon bladderworts, beaujolais cranberries, and crimson pitcher plants. Admired by every visitor to our house, it sat proudly in front of our living room window for months, reminding us of the bounteous life under the snow. Mom, an avid berry picker and co-lover of bogs, was delighted.

Islands

Newfoundland Island is affectionately known as the "rock," but the "rocks" would be more accurate. Scattered along our coastline are families of smaller islands spawned from the mother rock. They are essential components of our unique character.

Under sail and muscle power, our boats used these islands as springboards to the fishing grounds. Every kilometre that a man didn't have to row was a precious saving of energy and time. So, in almost every cove that provided reasonable shelter, small communities sprang up. Churches were built, children were schooled, lives were lived.

After gasoline and diesel power, the islands lost some of their advantage. Resettlement policies encouraged people to leave them in favor of more concentrated services.

Bay du Nord

The ecological prophets say that we have about twenty years left to protect our most vital natural areas. After that, it will be too late. As roads, transmission lines, mines, clear-cut logging, and other developments eat into our wilderness, by default we will have lost freedom to choose the best of wild Newfoundland and Labrador. Our economic agenda dictates that these developments occur, but our cultural and ecological well-being require that we also care for our wilderness.

For over fifteen years I have helped in the struggle to protect the places that really matter in the Province. Our progress has been painfully slow, but some gains have been made.

1990 was a landmark year. The Bay du Nord Wilderness Reserve was set aside—thirty-five thousand square kilometres of Newfoundland's best unspoiled country. It has one of the finest wild rivers left on the island and an extensive network of huge lakes where canoe paddles can quietly dip in wilderness splendor; extensive barrenlands where several

thousand woodland caribou thrive; thick, dark forests where the sound of a chain saw is alien; and vast wetlands where Canada geese congregate on the best breeding grounds of the island. It is a wild realm with an enduring landscape and fabric of life still largely unchanged.

ABOUT THE AUTHOR   DENNIS MINTY

Born in Twillingate, Newfoundland, Dennis Minty has been involved in environmental education and photography for most of his adult life. He is the author of two science textbooks and the author and photographer of two other books. He says, "I take pictures as an expression of my personal connection with the water, sky, land, and life that surrounds me." Dennis now lives in St. John's, Newfoundland.

A Musical Note

Whether my fingers are guided gently across the black and ivory keys of the piano, or whether they're reaching out to carefully lace up my worn leather jazz boots, music has brought such colorful tones to my life. Each time I set foot on a theatre stage or sit perched upon a piano bench to gaze upon a recital audience, I'm inspired by the overwhelming excitement stirred deep within me. Piano lessons have allowed me to explore the mysteries of classical music, while lessons in dance fulfill a passion to express the way music makes me feel. Music has brought such joy to my life, and when this day is through, I will once again rest my head upon a pillowcase adorned with musical notes and follow the words my mother so often says: "Dance into your dreams, Ashley!"

Ashley Buczkowski
Grade 6

I like writing because I can express all of my feelings when I am writing. I really enjoy writing about the things I love the most, so I wrote this paragraph about music because I want to show everyone how much fun music really is!

Ashley Buczkowski

Painting

Most artists paint when they have an emotion in their hearts. When artists are angry or excited, they will use colors like deep reds, oranges, or purples to represent this emotion. When they are happy, some artists will use light colors like pinks, yellows, or greens. Every artist is different, though, so different colors will show different feelings for each one. Feelings also determine different styles of painting. When feeling calm, an artist might paint a picture that is very simple. Intense colors like reds, oranges, or purples might suggest conflicting emotions. It is quite amazing how different artists help you feel what their emotions are with just a brush, some paint, and a canvas!

Maricia Fischer-Soran
Grade 6

I really enjoy writing because it is a way to express myself and to catch an audience's interest.

Alexander C. Bjornson

Music in My Life

My name is Alexander C. Bjornson. I am writing about the musical experience in my life.

In Grade 5, I was in an opera called Carmen. It was a thrilling sensation! Getting dressed in costumes, performing before an audience, meeting actors and actresses, and, oh, much more!!!

Today I still perform. I'm in the V. I. V. A. Boy's Choir, and just recently I was chosen to be in a television commercial. It was all very exciting! I love music, and I want to continue studying and performing it. It's fun and brings joy to life. LEARN TO LOVE IT!

Alexander C. Bjornson
Grade 6

LIBRARY
Meridian Heights School

GET SET FOR THE NET!

by Nyla Ahmad
Illustrations by
Stephen MacEachern

The Internet, or "Net" for short, is a world-wide network of computer networks. What's that? Think of a spider spinning its web. First the spider spins a few strands of silk joined in diamond-shaped sections. As the web grows, the sections are attached to more sections. On and on spider goes, building more sections and attaching them to the rest until, finally, the web is complete. The Internet is like a spider's web except that, instead of silk, the Internet "weaves" telephone lines to create sections of linked computers. Computer experts began creating the Internet by linking a few computers together to form a group, or network. Then they linked, or hooked up, this first network to other networks with cables, microwaves, satellites, and the other high-tech systems that carry electronic information around the world.

A spider's web houses one spider, but the Net's web of computers is home to more than forty million scientists, teachers, journalists, librarians, business people, and kids like you—and two million newbies (new

Internet users) add on every month. The Internet web is set up to catch information, not flies. All kinds of information—messages, books, photos, video, and sound—travel across the web in just a few seconds. And, just as a spider wanders around its web, walking along interconnected strands of silk, Internet users wander the worldwide web of computers to get at some incredible stuff.

History of a Hooked-Up World

The Internet is today's newest and fastest way to communicate with people around the world. But you know what? The technology that makes the Net possible isn't really new. Some brilliant thinkers throughout techno-history invented the telephones, radios, computers, and other stuff that the Internet needs to operate—and some were invented more than 150 years ago! Take a look at this survey of communication history to find out who the geniuses were and how their brainwaves affect us today.

1844

Morse invents the telegraph and sends the first electronic message.

Electronic Messages

Samuel Morse invented the telegraph in 1844. For the first time, words could travel rapidly over long distances, wherever telegraph wires could be strung. When its "key" was pressed, the telegraph transmitted an electric pulse over wires to another telegraph machine. Each pulse made a "dot" or a "dash" on a strip of paper in the receiving telegraph. These dots and dashes were called Morse Code, and were translated into the letters of the alphabet. More than one hundred years after the invention of the telegraph, the first computer was invented. The computer also transmits a code of pulses. But it does the code-to-letter translation automatically, and also has a "memory" where it can store data. You can still print a copy on paper, but only if you want to.

1946

The Electronic Numerical Integrator and Calculator (ENIAC) begins to operate.

1858

First transatlantic cable is laid, allowing intercontinental electric communication.

Going the Distance

Once messages could be transmitted instead of mailed, they could be sent farther and faster. A transatlantic cable beneath the Atlantic Ocean, between North America and Europe, was the start of intercontinental electric communication. The cable carried telegraph signals across the Atlantic in just minutes—instead of the three months a postal ship would take to carry letters the same distance. Nearly one hundred years later, people started to send messages around the globe through the air instead of under the ocean—with satellites. A satellite dish can send electronic signals up to a satellite orbiting 36 000 km above us in space. Space satellites then reflect, or bounce, these signals back down to Earth to other dishes around the globe—all within seconds.

1957

First satellite sends information back from space.

The first typewriter is invented. Things no longer need to be written by hand.

The Keys of Progress

Before the first typewriter was invented, everything that wasn't printed on a press had to be written out by hand. People spent weeks handwriting pages of text to be printed in newspapers, books, and other important documents. In 1867, a newspaper editor named Christopher Sholes invented the first fast and efficient way to put text on paper. He called it the typewriter. The "keys of letters" he invented got the whole world "typing." Nearly one hundred years after the first typewriter, the first computer network was created. With networked computers, a user can type a message onto the keyboard of one computer and have it appear on the screen of another computer. Typed messages can be sent instantly—without the use of a single piece of paper!

Scientists develop the first computer network to transmit messages electronically.

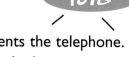

Bell invents the telephone. It sends the human voice over electronic wires.

Bells and Whistles

One invention really changed the way we communicate with each other, and we use it every day—it's the telephone. Alexander Graham Bell, perhaps one of the greatest inventors ever, created his first telephone back in 1876. For the first time, people could actually talk to someone far away. Today, more than 525 million telephones ring throughout the world, and more than 400 billion telephone conversations take place each year. The telephone lines that transmit voice messages from coast to coast are also the backbone of the Internet. Less than a hundred years had passed after Bell's first telephone conversation when the Internet was created to get computers "talking" to each other over telephone lines, no matter how far away or remote they might be.

The Internet starts sending messages between computers around the world.

1889

Edison's phonograph and Eastman's flexible photographic film are introduced.

Hear It, See It

Around 1889, two major inventions took place in sound and pictures. Thomas A. Edison, inventor of the light bulb, created the phonograph, a machine that could record and play sound. George Eastman, founder of Eastman-Kodak Co., created a photographic film that made way for the technology of modern cameras. As time went on, these two technologies began working together and advancing, so people could better hear and see what they recorded. By the turn of the century, motion pictures were invented, and television followed a few decades afterwards. Within one hundred years of the first major breakthroughs in pictures and sound, we were living in an audiovisual world. Today, audio and video data can be transmitted from one computer to another.

1994

Video and audio are transmitted over the Internet.

1894

Marconi develops the radio. It sends signals through the air without using wires.

A Wireless World

Guglielmo Marconi developed the radio back in 1894. It must have seemed like magic, as invisible signals travelled through the air from one radio antenna to another, allowing first the Morse Code and then voices to be heard loud and clear. This set the wireless world in motion! Today, a concert performer sings into a wireless microphone. Wireless microphones, and many other everyday devices, work with radio waves. Scientists say that by the year 2000, just over one hundred years after Marconi's first radio, a new wireless world may exist. The possibilities seem endless—video-conferencing, remote surgery, and virtual reality. We'll be able to get in touch with anyone, from anywhere in the world, without the need of a single plug, cable, or power socket.

2000

Experts predict a fully interactive system of communication, on-line and wireless.

Reality Byte

In the 1970s, the U.S. Defense Department began looking into computer networks. They realized that, for computers to understand each other, a network needed a standard "language." So they developed a language, called the Internet Protocol (IP). This made it possible for computers to chat it up on the Net.

Famous First Words

"WOW! It actually works!" That's what a scientist might have been thinking the first time an invention finally worked, but that's not what most of them said. Here are the first messages transmitted on breakthroughs in communications. Can you identify who sent what?

1. "What hath God wrought!"
2. "Europe and America are united by telegraphy. Glory to God in the highest, on Earth peace, and good will toward men."
3. "Mr. Watson, come here. I want you."
4. "Good morning, Mr. Edison. Glad to see you back. I hope you are satisfied with the kineto-phonograph."
5. "S"

(a) Sent by Thomas Edison's assistant
(b) Sent by Alexander Graham Bell
(c) First message to Marconi over the radio
(d) Sent by Samuel Morse
(e) First transatlantic message

Life Is a Highway

Take a look at a highway map of your country. You'll find a network of roads linking all the cities and towns to each other. Pick two destinations on your map (the further they are from each other the better) and see how many different ways—short or long, using big roads or small—you can find. Too many routes to count, right?

In many ways the Internet is like your highway map. The Net is home to computers instead of the towns and cities on your map. Telephone connections through wire, radio, or satellite "routes" are the highways and roads you travel to visit those distant locations. Just imagine how many millions of ways, long or short, you can take to get from a computer in St. John's to another in Singapore.

The good news for you is that you don't need a licence to drive on the I-Way. All you need is a computer, a modem, the right software, a host, and a telephone line. With these things, you can get on-line and blast off into cyberspace. Read on, and you'll find out all you need to know about gearing up, hooking up, and life on the I-Way!

Famous First Words
1.—(d); 2.—(e); 3.—(b); 4.—(a); 5.—(c)

32

Where Is Cyberspace?

Cyberspace is the high-tech zone that exists behind the flickering light of your computer screen, in the wires of your telephone line, and up in space between orbiting satellites. It's the "place" where digital bits of information—from your computer and from the forty million others on the Net—meet. It's not a physical place where you can go, like a city or park, but it's a place your computer can take you to. The term "cyberspace" was first used back in 1984 by author William Gibson in his sci-fi novel *Neuromancer*. Today, cyberspace is how most people describe the world of the Net. Just think of a telephone conversation—where do those chats really take place? They happen in the phone line that connects you and your pal. On the same digital map of the electronic universe, the computers on the Net chat it up in the far reaches of cyberspace!

Life on the I-Way

Take a trip down the I-Way and you'll find yourself zipping across phone lines, crossing over bridges, bouncing off of satellites, and flying across the world within seconds. To make it all happen, computer scientists and other experts use the latest in high-tech tools to create the fastest I-Way on Earth. Here's a map of the I-Way. To decode the icons on the map, just turn the page.

Host A host computer links a user's computer to the Internet. Many people can use the same host to get to the Net.

 User To get on the I-Way, your computer must be connected to a host computer. Then you become a Net user.

 Modem Your modulator-demodulator, or modem for short, sends signals from your computer and receives signals from other computers on the Net over phone lines.

 Phone Lines Information travels electronically in and out of your home through telephone cables.

 Trunk Lines Long-distance, high-speed digital connections are like the main highways of the I-Way. They link the phone companies working around the world together on the Net.

 Routers Like a post office, routers choose the best route to send your message.

 Packets Messages—digital text, pictures, or audio or video data—are broken up and travel on the Net in tiny packets. Packets travel between your computer and others on the Net.

 Messages Once they've reached their destination, tiny packets are reassembled in their correct order to be read as a message.

 TCP/IP Transmission Control Protocol/Internet Protocol is the communication standard used on the Net. All information on the Net must meet this protocol to be transmitted. Packets are checked for correct protocol throughout the Net.

 Error Packets that do not meet TCP/IP are sent back to you as an error. Your computer screen will show a message that the message wasn't sent.

 Satellites Signals zip up to a satellite in space and then are downlinked, or reflected, to a satellite dish back on Earth. Satellites make it easy to send and receive information quickly and smoothly around the globe.

 Bridges A bridge lets a user in one network "crossover" to another network on the Net.

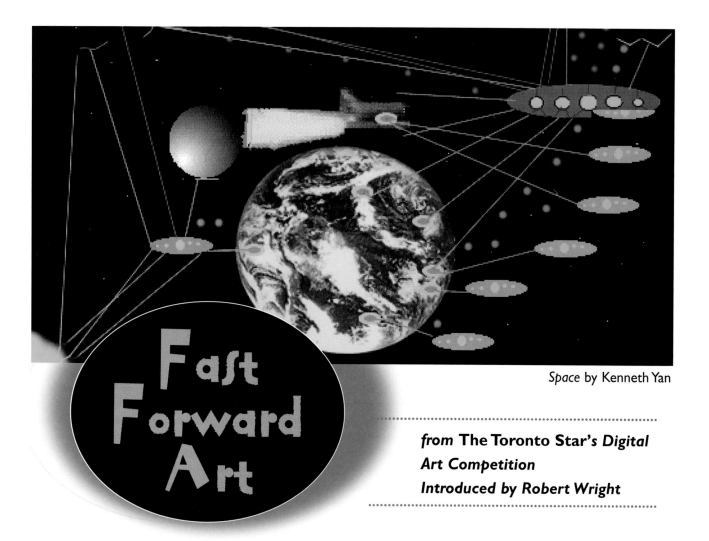

Space by Kenneth Yan

L ike beauty, art is in the eye of the beholder. Whether the creator uses pencil and paper, paint brush and canvas, or mouse and computer doesn't really matter. If the finished product is considered art by the viewer, it is art.

It is perhaps a sign of the times that many young people today are just as comfortable using the digital tools of the computer as their parents were using natural tools such as crayons and paint. Some are even more comfortable!

In some ways, working on a computer can make it harder for an artist to move from the stage of thinking of an artistic idea to actually creating it. For example, many people find it hard to draw with a mouse. Yet computers also present possibilities that

are wonderfully liberating; for example, the range of colors available to the artist. As the software and hardware become more complex and more affordable; child artists are presented with a virtually infinite palette of possibilities with which to work.

Will using computers produce better art than what was created before? Not necessarily, since art is a creative process, and the quality of the finished art depends on the quality of the original idea. But computer technology will certainly result in different art. This is demonstrated by the following selections chosen from among the entries in the "Under 13" category of the Fast Forward Digital Art Competition. Here are the paintings, with comments in the artists' own words.

Hinal Pithia — Age 6

Landscape

I love to paint the things of nature—trees, clouds, water, sun, apples falling on the grass. I love using the computer because I can use so many colors with my mouse. I wish I could have a color printer, though!

Peter M. Ponert, Jr. — Age 12

Adélian Aspiration

When I started my picture, I wanted to create something that was far-fetched, out of the ordinary. Adélie penguins live in the Antarctic. They are flightless birds, and their black and white feathers make them look as if they are wearing tuxedos. Adélie penguins are graceful swimmers, and seem to enjoy having fun as much as humans do. So I put together Adélie, the species of penguin, and aspiration (dream) to create "Adélian Aspiration"—a penguin's dream. With the help of my computer, my magic paint brush, I made this vision a reality. Creating it was loads of fun.

Kenneth Yan — Age 11

Space

Here's why I like creating digital art instead of art on paper. Normally, I do not like drawing. But when it comes to digital art, it's not so boring as drawing on paper. The eraser works with the click of the mouse. There are special options called "Lighting Effects" that can show a light, where the image is from dark to bright. There is also something that draws from one main color to another, which has all the different colors in between. This option is called "Gradients." I think I would be wasting a lot of time using a pencil, crayons, and paper!

Michelle M. Ponert   **Age 10**

Cool Cat

My inspiration for creating "Cool Cat" was to do something new with something old. I took the popularity of the cat and added a bit of a modern look. I like cats, and nobody has done this kind of art work before. I find the North Pole very interesting too, and thought it would make a unique picture. Creating this picture was fun, and a learning experience.

Keith Yan   **Age 8**

Underwater Picture

I like doing work on the computer better than doing it on paper because, first of all, it is a lot faster and easier because I can cut and paste. I can paint by just clicking once with my mouse and I can make shapes easily and accurately.

Larisa Storisteanu   **Age 12**

Untitled

I use MS Paint to do my art. I fill in details working at pixel-level in Zoom-in mode, sometimes for hours. I love the room for experimentation that's made possible by the computer. I have a passion for computer art—it's cool!

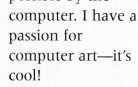

Arthur Lui   Age 13

Armyman

I drew a man in the army because I admire soldiers for the sacrifice they make when they fight for our country. I like to use the computer as a drawing medium because I've wanted to draw graphics for computer games. It is more difficult to draw with a mouse than with a pencil, but I like the challenge. Also, the picture can be modified and reproduced whenever I wish.

Laura Shaw   Age 12

The Tree

I drew this picture because I think the environment is really important and the tree represents nature. I like to use the computer while drawing and painting because I can "undo" any mistakes I make, make lots of changes, and experiment.

Tabitha Whiteside   Age 10

Missed Me

I was inspired to draw the "Missed Me" drawing because I had read an article on sharks recently. I figured that I should add a little humor to my drawing instead of just showing a fish behind a shark. I was also inspired by having some of my hand-drawn pictures published in *Owl* magazine before. The magazine ran a contest with the topic "If you discovered a new plant, what would it look like?" I sent them art on that topic, and it was published.

Hidden Horde

I was inspired to do this picture because I have always been fascinated with dragons, and drawing them in the computer gives them a unique effect. Just because things aren't real doesn't mean they can't be "brought to life" in a drawing, and with drawings you can share the experience with everyone. After all, a picture is worth a thousand words!

The Group

I love to draw people and animals, and this was one of my favorite pictures. Doing art on my Macintosh computer is easy. It's lots of fun to play with the drawing tools, the hundreds of colors and patterns.

The Group

And the winner is . . .

Easter Rabbit

I started off just drawing for fun, but now I love to create all kinds of art, using sculpture, water colors, crayons, Plasticine, or computer. Whatever works, I'll use. To create Easter Rabbit, I used Fractal Design Dabbler 1.0 on an Apple Mac computer.

The computer is just a different way of doing things. It's no easier or harder than other ways—just different. It's just another tool for creating art. I especially like creating art about animals and the environment.

World Shrinkers

by Lynn Bryan

Morgan video-conferencing with author Lyle Weis.

"It's amazing! It'll bring the world so much closer together!" That's what people said when the telephone and television were invented. But that was just the beginning for communication technology. Now, there's also e-mail, the Internet, faxes, and video-conferencing. Today, kids are fast becoming knowledgeable users of these new communication systems. Here's your chance to check out two projects in which kids use technology to shrink the distances between themselves and others.

Project Interact

Take enthusiastic students in schools distant from one another, interested teachers, a professional writer, and computer terminals hooked together for video, and what do you get? Project Interact—students coming together on-line with other students and with author Lyle Weis, to share and edit their writing. A visit with Grade 6 students at Minchau School shows how it works. Let's listen in on an editing session.

Lyle: Have a look at the part I've just underlined and see what you could do to describe the mountains more vividly.

Morgan: Maybe I could write, The mountains stand higher than the clouds.

Lyle: I think that would be excellent. Just type that phrase you're suggesting on the whiteboard beside your poem. That way we won't forget it.

That's part of a conversation between Lyle Weis and Morgan, a student at Minchau School, as they work together on her poem. Morgan is sitting in front of her computer at school, but Lyle is at home in his study. His voice is coming from the computer, and his picture is on the screen in one of the photo windows there. Morgan's picture is in the other photo window and her poem is displayed on a part of their screens called the whiteboard.

All of this is done using video-conferencing software and miniature cameras set up beside each of their computers. This setup allows Lyle Weis to help students revise and edit their writing in a personal and interesting way—but from a distance.

As she and Lyle work together on her poem, they can use different features of the software program. Lyle can use a drawing tool to underline, circle, or cross out words or chunks of Morgan's writing. He can also make arrows to show where to move a line or word. These revising and editing marks appear on their whiteboards or display boards, along with any suggested changes or notes they type

there. The conferencing program allows Morgan and Lyle to carry on a written conversation by typing their messages in a boxed portion of the screen called a chatboard, or they can click on "Push To Talk" and speak into the microphone. If all this sounds like fun, it is. But it's also serious, focused revising and editing.

At the end of her session with Lyle, Morgan makes sure she saves all the whiteboard editorial comments and markings onto her diskette. That way, she can refer to them when she does further revising and editing on her own or with peers. At that time she can work right on the screen or print out a hard copy.

Morgan's next editing session might be on-line with a student in McCauley School, the school that Minchau is paired

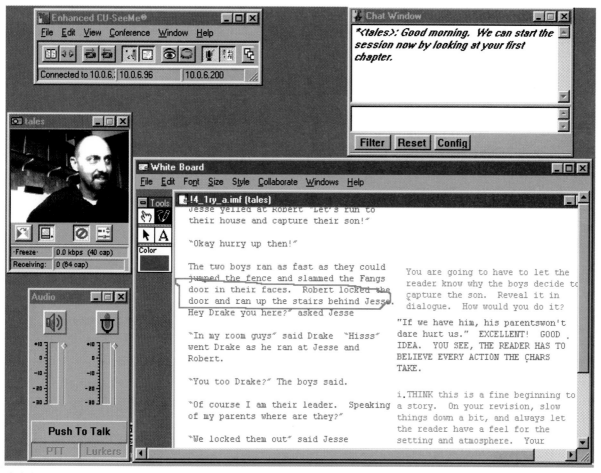

Lyle Weis on-screen with whiteboard of another editing session.

with in Project Interact. The Minchau kids share their writing with student partners at McCauley using exactly the same technology and procedures as they use when working with Lyle Weis. Student-to-student conferences tend to be a bit more chatty than the sessions with Lyle. Tim explains. "Our student partners at McCauley are kids like us. They think like us and we're doing a lot of the same things, so have a lot to talk about when we look at our poems."

Which kind of conference is most useful? The students see value in both. About working with the professional writer, Tim says, "Lyle can give us really great advice. He knows a lot about writing because he's been doing it for years, and he's good." What about their peer editors? Ashley, another student at Minchau, comments that student editors are particularly good at pointing out things that don't make sense and asking you to check your spelling.

As they gain more experience, student editors will be able to focus on more aspects of writing. "Now we're working together to find words that will help people visualize what we're saying in our poems. Really, that's the big part of writing," says Ryan.

Ashley realizes how lucky they are to be able to video-conference. "Lyle would never have time to come out to all our schools, but he can look at our poems on disk. And all of us kids sure couldn't get together from all over the place to help each other," she says. "So video-conferencing gives us editing input we couldn't get in any other way."

Keypals

Where in the world is Port Fairy? Students in Mr. Milson's class at Good Shepherd School in Edmonton, Alberta, not only know the answer to that question, they also know how to get there in just a few seconds! Port Fairy is halfway around the world from Edmonton, down on the southeastern tip of Australia, in the state of Victoria. It takes about seventeen hours to fly there and around two weeks for a letter to arrive. But a message sent by e-mail arrives almost instantly. Incredible, isn't it?

The Grade 6 students at Good Shepherd think it's exciting, too. Through e-mail they have keypals in Australia—kids they write to using a computer keyboard instead of pen and paper. On days when the e-mail comes in and they get a printout of their letters, the students can hardly wait to read messages from their own keypals and then listen while some of the other kids' keypal letters are read aloud.

Checking out e-mail from Australia.

Sarah writing to her
new Australian friends.

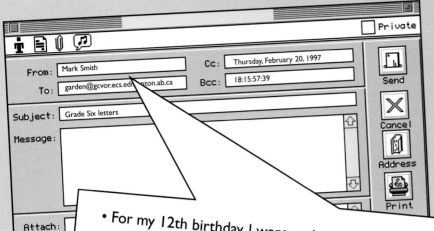

From: Mark Smith   Cc: Thursday, February 20, 1997

To: garden@gcvor.ecs.edm...ton.ab.ca   Bcc: 18:15:57:39

Subject: Grade Six letters

Message:

Attach:

• For my 12th birthday, I went scuba diving. I saw about 20 anemones with orange centres and white tentacles. I touched one. It was sticky.

• Last weekend, my family and I went to a place called Lorne, which is another town by the sea. Have you ever been to the beach? We go there all the time because Dad is on a surf boat rowing team. He is in Port Fairy S.L.S.C (Surf Life Saving Club). We went there for a surf carnival.

• Do you like whales? I love them. There is a town called Warrnambool and whales come there every May to give birth. There is a whale that comes there regularly called Dorothy.

• On Friday I went over to a friend's house to stay the night. We rode a motor bike over to the next-door neighbour's house and played Markers Up for an hour and a half.

• There's not much happening lately, except last Wednesday we all had our Rubella needles. It didn't hurt because Mr. Pepperdine was stuffing us with lollies, and it took our mind off it.

• What type of novels do you like to read? I like to read ones by Paul Jennings and Morris Gleitzman. They're both famous Australian authors, so you might not know much about them.

• Hi. I live in Port Fairy at Black-Wood Road, Greenacres. We have just moved there. We used to live in a caravan park.

• I will be going to America on Friday, April the 18th. We leave here at 11:00 a.m. on Friday and get to America at 10:30 a.m. on the 17th of April. Sounds weird, doesn't it? That's the International Date Line for you!

• This week, I have to feed our next-door neighbour's emus. There are seven altogether. There are four chicks and three adults. It takes about five minutes every day and this morning when I went to feed them I saw two foxes. One of the adult emus dances.

• A couple of weeks ago the Port Fairy Folk Festival was held. Heaps of performers from all over the world came to play music. I went to see a band called Yothu Yindi. They are an Australian Aboriginal band that play didgeridoos and rhythm sticks. They also play guitars and drums and keyboards.

Kelly sending e-mail.

Often the keypals' correspondence focuses on their families, friends, pets, birthdays, and things they like to do, for they really want to get to know one another. However, there's lots more to share as well. Kelly mentions that kids in Port Fairy seem particularly interested in finding out about West Edmonton Mall and Canadian winters. They ask, "Is your mall really the biggest one in the world? What is snow like? How do you survive the cold weather?"

In their reply letters, students at Good Shepherd answer such questions, tell about themselves, and ask about things sparked by their keypals' letters. They might want to ask about a didgeradoo, or wonder what a lolly is, or how to play the game of Markers Up. Other kids suggest questions such as, "What weather disasters do you have?" What kind of music do you listen to?" "Have you ever seen a baby koala being born?" "How big are your spiders— because I don't really like spiders."

The students are very interested in the animals in each others' countries because they are so different. "I'd sure like to know more about wallabies, emus, dingos, wombats, and kookaburras," says Matthew. Then he adds, grinning, "And I want to ask if kangaroos really do box." Matthew suggests that kids in Australia would probably be interested in learning about Canadian animals like beavers, grizzly bears, and wolves. To share this information, the students plan to write reports and send them by e-mail as attached documents. That means the reports can be downloaded and printed out just like the actual e-mail letter.

Not everything can be shared through e-mail, though. Sometimes the students have to revert to snail mail—that's the Internet term for regular mail. Slow as it is, snail mail does provide a way for them to exchange packages containing things like pins, coins, hockey and baseball cards, photos, and friendship bracelets. As well, the classes are planning to make audio and video tapes to add an extra dimension to what they're learning about each other. It'll be fun to actually see how a certain game is played and to chuckle over each others' accents.

What other communication projects lie ahead for the keypals and the students of Project Interact? Perhaps they'll soon be able to exchange faxes and get together in wider video-conferences. Maybe they'll even create web sites to display their work and reach out to keypals and writers around the world. Who knows—some of these world shrinkers may even get to meet in person some day!

Fax Facts

by E.M. Hunnicutt
Illustrated by Leanne Francon

I ran to catch up with Hatch Peabody after school. "My parents got a fax machine for their home office!" I told him. "Just yesterday!"

"That's exciting, Barney," said Hatch.

"Right!" I said. "Written communication at the push of a button! Speed! Accuracy! You want to come over and see it work?" I couldn't wait to get home.

But Hatch didn't look excited. He looked worried. "Just don't forget the band has to play a gig Saturday."

"Hey! Make sense!" I yelled. "How can I forget with posters all over town saying, 'Music by The Mathematics, Saturday Night, School Gym?'" We're a rock trio. Hatch and I play guitar. Our buddy Matt plays drums.

"Barney, everybody knows how much you like high-tech stuff. If you start playing around with the fax, you won't memorize the words to our new song."

"Play around?!" I yelled. "Play! A fax machine isn't some little kid's video game, Hatch." I didn't tell him that the night before I'd faxed my MP, suggesting a shorter school year.

I'd also answered a few ads on TV. They'd faxed me instructions for raising rabbits, a recipe for grape jelly, and sixteen ways to glamorize my home with curtains and drapes.

But I wasn't playing around. You need to use a new piece of equipment to get used to it. "This is only Thursday," I told Hatch. "I've got three days to memorize those words. I already know the music."

"Four verses," Hatch reminded me. He didn't want to come over, but he did jot down my fax number.

On the way home, I saw a sign in a restaurant window. Guess what? A lot of restaurants will fax you their menus.

I had eight menus by the time my sister wandered into the office carrying her boom box and bringing me a sandwich. She saw the menus. "You must be hungry!" She had to shout over the sound of her music.

I *was* hungry. I'd skipped supper. "Thanks!" I yelled. "That sandwich looks great!"

"It's from Mom! She says you're starving. I say you're weird!"

I think my sister said something nice to me once. But it was years ago, back when she was learning to talk, so I can't be sure.

She turned to go, doing that silly jig she does to her music, but just then the song ended and the DJ said: "We're here to play the music you love! Call in your requests. Or, if you've moved into the electronic age, you can fax them in."

I don't know if he actually played any of the song requests I faxed. My radio's up in my room and I didn't want to leave the office, in case something came in.

Then Dad poked his head in the door. "Barney, just remember, the cost of the fax goes on the phone bill."

"Hey, Dad! I know this stuff. I'm the one who taught you to program the VCR, remember?"

Then the phone rang. "For you, Barney!" Mom called, and I picked up in the office.

It was Hatch. "Are you learning the song?"

"Look, I'm pretty busy here," I told him. A fax had started coming in. "I have to hang up."

It was a junk fax, an advertisement someone sends you without asking. Some people don't like junk faxes because they can tie up your machine and use up your paper—but, hey! I believe in communication. The fax told me my sheep would grow more wool if I air-conditioned my barns. I faxed back, "Send more information on sheep barns at your earliest convenience."

The phone rang again. Dad picked it up. "It's for you, Barney!"

This time it was Matt. "I'm having trouble learning the new song," he said. "The words are tricky. How about I come over and we work on it together?"

"Hatch put you up to this, didn't he? I bet Hatch said, 'Matt, phone old goof-off Barney and light a fire under him!'"

"He didn't say that," Matt protested. "Those weren't his exact words."

Then Hatch sent me a fax with—what else!—the words to the song in big capital letters. He'd gone out to a drugstore and PAID MONEY to send me a fax—but that sheet of paper gave me an idea. "Thank you, Hatch!" I said to no one. I was pretty sure I'd get the song memorized, but if I didn't, I could tape Hatch's fax to the back of my amp—and just read off the words.

I devoted the entire next evening to weather. This was Friday. I'd found a weather service that updated the forecasts every hour—more often in bad weather. It was a service for pilots. Sure, there was a small charge—but hey! Good stuff doesn't come free, and weather information is valuable. There was a storm brewing out west of us, so in one night I got twenty-two faxes!

As we set up our gear to play on Saturday, I tried to keep out of Hatch's way so he wouldn't start asking questions. I'd never actually gotten around to learning the song. I'd given my sister a ride to the dance, and when no one was looking, I had her tape the fax with the words to the song to the back of my amp. Then I pretended to be looking out at the gym decorations. "Wow! That's really great. Crepe paper in the school colors!"

"What's with you, Barney?" Matt asked. "It's *always* crepe paper in the school colors."

As we played, I was careful not to look at my amp and draw attention to that sheet of paper.

The new song came at the end of the first set. Matt did a little roll on the drums, and I looked down at my amp—and read, SHOWERS PROVINCE-WIDE, TEMPERATURES MID TEENS. I'd grabbed the wrong fax! I was dead—stone cold dead in the water!

Then I heard Hatch talking to the audience. "Something different tonight, kids! An old-fashioned sing-a-long!" He went off-stage and came back carrying a poster two metres square. He'd printed out the words to the song so they could be read by the audience—and by ME! Sometimes your friends know you so well, it's scary. If Hatch was sending me a message, I sure got it.

I had plenty of time to think things through. I had to go to work part-time in a supermarket for two months to pay my part of the phone bill. When you bag groceries, there's not a lot to think about—in between asking, "Do you want your milk in a bag?" and "Paper or plastic?"

Computers can age it, change it, morph it, or rearrange it. They're high-tech masters ...

In Your FACE

by Elizabeth MacLeod

What's in a Face?

Let's face it—your face is more than just a place for your nose, eyes, and mouth. The front of your head is your physical identity card. No two people have exactly the same face. Identical twins come pretty close to having the same looks, but even their faces aren't exactly alike. And, each person's face is made up of two different sides. Take a look at the three photos on the right. Only one of the three shots is actually what the kid looks like. The other two photos are made-up faces using his two left, or two right, sides. Can you guess which one's which? So what's in a face? Well . . . it's filled with bone structure, facial features, and tonnes of other stuff that makes you look like you!

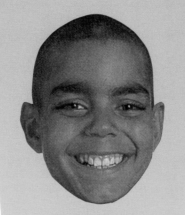

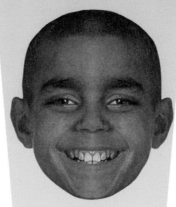

Place That Face

"Hey, that's the guy on TV!" When you spot a familiar face you're not looking at specific features, like a nose or ears, you're noticing the whole face with all its parts. That's why witnesses to a crime find it hard to describe the specific details of a criminal's face, but they may be able to spot the bandit in a police line-up. Computers are designed to recognize faces in the same way humans do. They analyze all the parts of a face and translate it into digital code. This way, a computer can "see" a face and then match it to a person. TV companies may one day use the system to find out exactly who is watching their shows. So, the next time you tune in to the tube, watch out—a computer may be tuning in to you!

In Japan, couples can scan their faces into a computer that predicts what their future kids might look like.

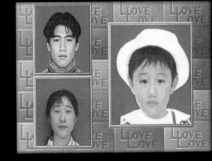

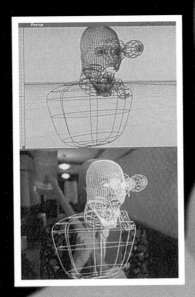

Computer magic can turn movie actors into cartoon characters that look and act amazingly real.

Mighty Morphin' Faces

If you've been to the movies lately, you've probably seen some amazing special effects. In *The Mask,* for instance, animators used high-tech computer programs and techniques to make Jim Carrey's eyes pop out of his head and his jaw drop to his belly button. Using morphing and digital warping programs, animators can make faces and whole bodies do almost anything. One secret animators use to make weird new faces look as realistic as possible is to do a lot of touching-up, especially around the eyes and mouth. Why? Because they know those are the areas people really look at when they look at faces. If animators can make the eyes and mouth look right, then the face will look real, too. Fooled you!

One-quarter of all your muscles are in your face and neck.

The fastest muscle in your body is the one that makes your eyelids open and close.

There are fourteen bones in your face and over one hundred muscles.

Your lips are red because your skin there is so thin that you can see the flesh underneath it.

Your thinnest skin is in your eyelids.

Your lower jaw is the only bony part of your face that moves.

50

Growing Up Fast

Want to know what you'll look like in a few years? A computer-aging program could tell you. All it needs is a recent photo of your face. Computer programs—designed with information from dentists, anthropologists, and plastic surgeons—measure up to fifty facial features such as chin shape and the space between the eyes. Then, the computer can estimate how these dimensions will change as your face grows. Aging children is more difficult than aging adults because kids' faces change more quickly. To get the best results, experts look at kids' parents, brothers, and sisters to see if there's a family pattern. Police can use this system to create current images of criminals who have been on the run for a few years or of kids who have been missing for a long time.

Photos of family members and a computer-aging program are used to figure out what this five-year-old will look like at the age of eight.

A Change of Face

Change your eyes, nose, hair, even change your face! Hairdressers and make-up artists can display your face on a computer screen to try out future "looks." Scientists can use the system to travel back in time by reconstructing ancient skulls. This Egyptian mummy (left) lived three thousand years ago. Today's modern technology helps us see what she looked like back then!

An interactive computer program called FaceNet lets you rearrange your looks. First, you stand in front of a computer that's hooked up to a video camera that captures an image of your face. Then, with the press of a button, the distortion begins!

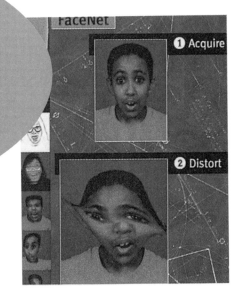

Faceports Please!

In the future, your passport may carry a special number that describes your face. Where does the number come from? First, a black-and-white photo of your face is translated into digital code. Then, a computer checks your facial measurements, like the distance between your mouth and eyes, which is unique to each person. This information is converted into a single number, which becomes the number on your passport. A customs officer could scan your face with a special tool and compare it to the number on your passport. In seconds, the computer will know if it's really you. Attention travellers: Show your faceports, please!

Meet Emily of New Moon

by Catherine Rondina

Have you ever wondered what it would be like to be a television actor, maybe even the star of your own series? Well, that's exactly what happened to Martha MacIsaac, of Charlottetown, Prince Edward Island. She was discovered by a film company and hired to play Emily Starr, the title role in the television series Emily of New Moon. *The series is based on the Emily books by Canadian author Lucy Maud Montgomery. Here's what twelve-year-old Martha has to say about her exciting new career.*

CR: Martha, had you ever done any acting before you got the part in *Emily of New Moon?*

MM: A little. When I was six, I played one of the Avonlea children in a production of *Anne of Green Gables.* Then, the summer between Grade 5 and Grade 6, I did some commercials for P.E.I. Tourism. I was ten years old then.

CR: How did you get that job, and what did you do in the commercials?

MM: My mom saw the job advertised in the newspaper, and took me down for an audition. I played an ordinary kid on a beach. My line was, "Come play on my island!"

CR: And how old were you when you did the *Emily of New Moon* series?

MM: I was eleven, going on twelve, when we started shooting. I was in Grade 7.

CR: How did you get that part?

MM: It was because of the commercials I'd done. One of the series producers, Marlene Matthews, was in P.E.I. looking for actors. She spoke to someone at the P.E.I. Tourism Board, who recommended me. So Marlene phoned me. I went and had breakfast with her, and then she took me to an audition.

CR: Were you nervous at the audition?

MM: No, not at all. I didn't even have to read the part. It was just a getting-to-know-you meeting. Quite a few young actors showed up for the audition. Afterwards, the producers decided which of us they wanted to call back, and gave us a script to memorize.

CR: Then you had a second audition, right?

MM: Right. That was neat. They flew me and my mom all the way to Toronto for the audition. I wasn't scared. I'm not a shy person at all, so it was fun.

CR: How did you react when you heard you got the part?

MM: They phoned me. My friend Jessie was at my house and when I hung up the phone I yelled, "I got the part!" and we started jumping up and down and screaming.

CR: What were some of the things you liked about being part of a television cast?

MM: Everything! My very favorite thing was the people I got to meet. They were so kind and thoughtful.

CR: Did the adult actors help you with your acting?

MM: Yes. If there was a hard scene to memorize they would ask the director if they could wait awhile, and they would go over the scene with me a few times. Or if I forgot a line, they would help me.

CR: Did you find it hard to memorize your lines? Did you forget a lot?

MM: No. I have a pretty good memory, and knowing that someone would cue me if I forgot helped me relax. So I didn't forget many lines.

CR: What was it like working with the director?

MM: There was a different one for each episode. Directors tell you what to do—how and where to move—and give you directions about your acting. It was easy to do what they wanted.

CR: Was one of your parents on the set with you while you were filming?

MM: No. I wouldn't really like them to be there because it would make me a little nervous.

CR: Were there many other kids on the set?

MM: Besides me, there were Jane Hennesey, Jessica Pellerin, and Sean

Roberts. Jane Hennesey is my double and stand-in for the Emily character, so she was there with me every day. She tried out for a part in *Emily,* and when they saw how much alike we looked, she got the part of the Emily stand-in. That means she stands in for me while the crew is setting up shots. Jessica Pellerin played Ilse Burnley in the series, and Sean Roberts played Teddy Kent. Oh, yes, and Kris Lemche played Perry Miller. But he really isn't a kid—he's eighteen.

CR: Is there anything you didn't like about working on the show?

MM: You sure have to get used to getting up early! They would come and pick me up at around 7:00 in the morning, so I had to be all ready to go.

CR: Where was the show filmed?

MM: At Summerside, on the Island. We filmed in an old airplane hangar.

CR: Is Summerside close to where you live?

MM: No, it's about one hour away, so I had to stay in a hotel in Summerside during the week. We worked out a whole schedule so that I always had someone to stay with me overnight. My mom would stay with me at the hotel one night a week, my dad on another night, and my tutor on Wednesday nights. Every Thursday night I'd stay with Sheila McCarthy, one of the adult actors. Then on Friday I'd go home to Charlottetown.

CR: What was your average day like when you were filming the series?

MM: Well, as I said, they would pick me up at 7:00. I would go to the set and talk to people for awhile. Then I'd put on my costume, and get my hair and make-up done. After that, I'd rehearse the scene I had to do. Then, while the film crew set up the scene I would go to school on the set. It was in a room in the same building. Jane Hennesey would stand in for me while I studied. When it was time to film the scene, I would go back to the set. After that it would be lunch time. After lunch, I'd go back to have my hair and make-up touched up. All afternoon I'd go back and forth between the set and school. I usually got back to the hotel around 6:30 because I liked to stay around the set and talk to people.

CR: What was it like going to school on the set?

MM: They had a tutor, and all of us kids from the show went to her between takes. She was really nice, and she sure knew a lot— she taught us all our subjects. I liked going to school on the set, but it's really different from regular school. Some days we'd be tutored for two or three hours, and other days not at all. It all depended on the filming schedule. So I was a bit worried that I'd fall behind the kids in my class at school. But I've got my marks back now, and I did just fine. When I went back to my regular school I was up to level with everyone else.

CR: Did you miss other things about not going to regular school?

MM: Not really. Of course, I missed my friends, but Jane Hennesey, the girl who was my stand-in, became my best friend in the whole world. She was right there on the set with me every day, and that was great!

CR: How long did it take to film the series?

MM: We shot from September to January, and it was every day, Monday to Friday.

CR: With such a busy schedule, did you have time to do other things?

MM: I mostly just hung out with my friends on weekends. I also took singing lessons.

CR: What about your family? How did your being in the series affect them?

MM: Well, I didn't get to see my family much while we were filming. Just on the weekends. My mom and dad had to take days off work so they could be with me in Summerside overnight. But they are still glad I got the part.

CR: Do you have brothers and sisters?

MM: I have three sisters. Jane is the oldest, then Jill, then Sally and me. They like my being in the series too. My oldest sister Jane says she's proud of me.

CR: What do your friends think about your being an actor?

MM: They don't treat me any differently than before. I guess they got used to my being on TV because of the P.E.I. commercials. Actually, it's adults who ask me all kinds of questions about being in the series.

CR: Are you glad you got the part? Has being in the series made you think about acting as a career?

MM: I'm really glad I got the part. Yes, I'd like to be a professional actor. My dream is to go to Stratford, Ontario, to the Stratford Festival, and act there.

CR: Have you taken any acting lessons?

MM: Not since I did the series. I took some acting at a school after I did the tourism commercials, though.

CR: Now that you've been in a series yourself, do you notice different things when you watch TV or movies?

MM: Yes. I notice how they do certain special effects, and now I know how long it takes to do things on the set. Another neat thing is when I'm watching a show and I see someone I know from our show. Once I was watching *Seinfeld* and I saw Stephen McHattie, the actor who played Cousin Jimmy in the *Emily* series. I went, "Hey, wow!"

CR: Who are your favorite actors?

MM: I like Rosie O'Donnell, Robin Williams, and Sheila McCarthy— she played Aunt Laura on the show. She's a great actor.

CR: What's next for you, Martha?

MM: Well, we're going to film a second series of *Emily* starting in the summer. I'm really looking forward to that. Also, I'm auditioning for my first movie this spring.

CR: That sounds terrific. So, do you have any advice for other kids who would like to get into acting?

MM: If you think you'd enjoy it, get out there and try it!

CR: Thank you for taking the time to talk to me, Martha.

Fax Facts

There once was a student named Jax
Who sent in his homework by fax.
But Jax made a blunder
And got the wrong number.
The lesson is—check your fax facts.

Tara Gordon
Grade 6

Ways to Communicate

Code
On-line
Musically
Morse code
Using sign language
Numbers
In Braille
Computer language
Artistically
Talking
Extra sensory perception

Telephone
Objects
Gestures
Entertainment
Touch
Hieroglyphics
Exercise
Radio waves

Ashley Fix
Grade 6

Mark Lampert

I picked this topic because it is very interesting to me. I also picked it because I and many others use the Internet everyday.

Log On

"Beep-Beep-Pshshsh." The sound of Alex Stark going on the Internet.

One night Alex was surfing the Internet, as he did every night. When he looked up he gasped, as a message was flashing on his screen stating "YOU HAVE DISAPPEARED!" Alex searched the file, trying to find out where it came from. *Nothing.* He found *nothing.*

The next morning he was reading the newspaper when he read the headlines: ALEX STARK LAST SEEN IN FRONT OF HIS COMPUTER—POLICE HAVE NO LEADS. Alex had to get to the bottom of this, so he logged on to his computer. A minute passed when another message appeared. Appearances can be deceiving! Alex thought to himself. I'm a master at this game—I can do it! He started typing. Three hours passed and Alex was becoming tired. He jumped up and yelled, "Eureka!" He had found a way to write back to the mysterious person.

Moments after he sent the message he got one back:
SO IT IS SO,
YOU NOW KNOW.
THE NEWSPAPER WASN'T FROM A STORE,
I PUT IT AT YOUR DOOR.
GOOD JOB, OLD PAL!

Alex spent years trying to figure out who wrote the letters, but the person still remained anonymous. Eventually Alex forgot about it, until one night he got another message on his computer: I'M BACK!

Mark Lampert
Grade 6

these are the same in many different cultures around the world. Others vary with each culture. Symbolic gestures such as beckoning or nodding have a fixed meaning in each culture, but often vary from one part of the world to another. For example, most people in North America nod their heads to mean "yes," but in countries like Turkey and Iran, that same nod means "no."

So, what is unintentional body language? It's all the little movements and gestures we make without thinking about them. Researchers call these body language *cues*. They often send very clear signals, just like your friend's downcast eyes and drooping shoulders. Many cues depend on which culture people live in. Another important point to remember about cues is that context counts. In some situations, rubbing your nose may indicate your response to a situation. Of course, if you just have an itchy nose, it doesn't mean anything more than that!

Face Up to It

You can show more expression with your face than with any other part of your body—move your eyelids and eyebrows, wrinkle your forehead, or change the way you hold your mouth or chin. One very common body language cue is what researchers call the eyebrows flash. When people see someone they like they often quickly raise and lower their eyebrows once and smile. It's how a lot of us say "Glad to see you!" The way people move their eyes sends signals too. Shifting your eyes rapidly from side to side sends the message "I don't want to be here!" So does staring into the air or down at the ground. Looking away when someone is talking to you sends the message "I'm not really sure about what you're saying."

Another kind of message our faces send is what researchers call *gaze behavior*. Many people in North America consider it rude to stare at others. Instead, people glance at each other and look away repeatedly as they speak together. People who gaze deeply into each other's eyes are usually being very loving—or very aggressive. If you do sneak a look at someone and are caught staring, "eye etiquette" requires you to look quickly away. This sends the message "I did look, but I'm really not trying to dominate you."

TRY THIS

Tell someone a joke or funny story with a deadpan expression, and watch how your listener reacts; then try it with another listener, using animated facial expressions. Compare the results you get.

Acting Up

Arms and hands send many messages too. Although some of these cues are the same worldwide, they will not necessarily be the same for all cultures. Here in North America, crossing your arms in front of your chest often means "I am resisting you." Scratching or rubbing your nose (unless it is itchy) often signals doubt or puzzlement, especially if you are listening to someone. Rubbing the back of your neck can mean that you're feeling frustrated or angry, and locking your hands behind your head signals "I am superior" or "I'm in charge here."

Legs and feet send messages of their own. Crossing your legs when you're sitting down sends the same message of resistance as crossing your arms. Waggling your feet, or tapping one on the floor, signals that you want to get up and leave. The direction your legs or feet are pointed when you're sitting down shows the direction you are most interested in. If it's toward an exit, it means "Let me out of here!"

TRY THIS

Regulators are body language cues that respond to another person's speaking, or try to control it. Have someone talk to you about something, or read something aloud, glancing up frequently. First use body language cues to encourage the speaker to go on. Use ideas from this article, or just make the kind of movement you would make if you felt really interested. After a few minutes, start sending signals that you would like the speaker to stop. Later, ask your partner about which signals were noted, and how the speaker felt in response.

Posture and body position are part of the signalling system too. Slumped or drooping posture signals that the person is tired, or feels unhappy or inferior. It sends the message "Leave me alone." Tilting your head to one side often signals interest in what someone is saying, and so does leaning forward when you are sitting down. Leaning away or turning the body away signals lack of interest. People also use cues to send positive messages to their friends. When you copy, or echo, your friends' gestures and postures, you signal that you think and feel alike.

TRY THIS

The next time you are watching a TV program or a movie, check out how the actors use body language to signal meaning. Do the messages they send with their body language match up with the words they say, or are they at odds? How does this affect the way you "get" the message?

Spaced Out

Have you ever felt really uncomfortable when someone stood too close to you? That's because many people in North America are fussy about the amount of distance they keep between themselves and other people. Only relatives or close friends are welcome inside our inner space zone. Anyone else who comes this close may seem "pushy." On the other hand, if you keep too far away from someone you know well, you may seem "standoffish."

Personal Space Zones in North America

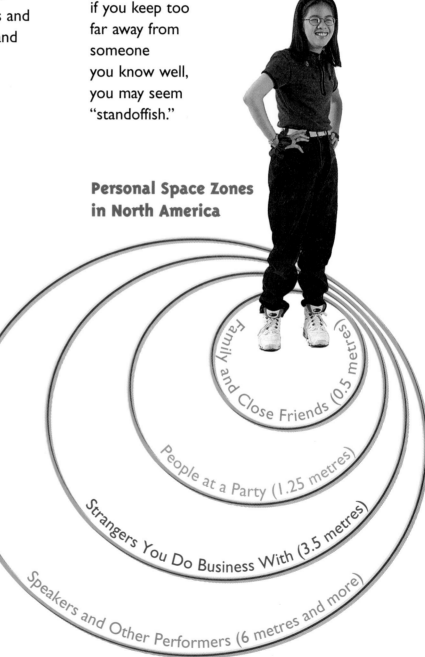

Family and Close Friends (0.5 metres)

People at a Party (1.25 metres)

Strangers You Do Business With (3.5 metres)

Speakers and Other Performers (6 metres and more)

When people feel their space is invaded, they often feel stressed, and use body language cues to signal their discomfort. Restless movements are one signal—stepping back, crossing and re-crossing the legs, foot tapping, and. hunching the shoulders. Crossing your body with one arm by fiddling with a watch or bracelet is another really clear signal that you're not at ease. What happens on a crowded elevator or subway, though? People packed together signal that they know they're too close, but they just can't help it. They avoid eye contact, and sit or stand stiffly, never leaning on the person next to them. People sitting side by side will cross their legs away from each other.

Sometimes people's body language cues send a false message. The way they act doesn't show how they're really feeling. Scientists call this *masking*. For example, someone who feels nervous might go around wearing a fixed, all-purpose smile. It sends the signal "Everything is fine with me." What it really means is "I look as if I agree with you, so please don't bother me."

Mostly, though, people's body language is one of the best ways to learn about them. So why not become a people-watcher, and learn to listen with your eyes?

TRY THIS

Observe through the day how close you stand to different categories of people. How close do you sit or stand to your family and friends? How about people you don't know as well? Does anybody come too close for comfort? If so, how do you feel, and what do you do?

Dancing the Cotton-Eyed Joe

by Joann Mazzio
Illustrated by France Brassard

I've been coming to country-western dances at Lake Valley since I was a baby. As soon as I was big enough to walk, I was trying to dance. I'm eleven now and I've learned the two-step, the waltz, and the polka. I've even learned to dance the schottische.

But until one night in January, I didn't know how to dance the Cotton-Eyed Joe. On the night I learned that dance, I learned something else, too.

On that winter night, the air in Lake Valley was like black velvet. That's because Lake Valley is a ghost town. No one lives there. But then, at 8:30 sharp, my dad turned on the lights in the old brick schoolhouse. It was like magic. Light streamed from the windows, and you could see people gathered outside the building. All kinds of folks come to the Saturday night dances—old people, young couples, and families with babies. In the shadows around the building were cars, RVs, and pickups splattered with mud from ranch roads.

Mrs. Jessup and Mrs. Taylor sat at the door collecting admission. I was carrying the pot of baked beans Mom had given me to take inside the schoolhouse.

I put the beans down at the entrance and stuck out my hand to be stamped. I don't have to pay admission because my mom and dad are in the band. But ever since I was a little kid, Mrs. Jessup or Mrs. Taylor has been stamping the back of my hand so that it says "Lake Valley Dance." It's like a ticket saying you've paid.

Mrs. Taylor said, "Well, Mark, have you learned to dance the Cotton-Eyed Joe yet?"

"No, Mrs. Taylor," I said. "I'm waiting for you to teach me."

"Oh, if it weren't for this arthritis in my knees, I'd have you dancing it in no time."

"That's right, Mark," Mrs. Jessup said. "That was Eula's specialty. If I didn't have this dad-blamed walker, I'd teach you myself."

"Have a good time tonight, honey," said Mrs. Taylor.

At the north end of the long room stood a table for the food people had brought. I dodged through the crowd to put our baked beans there.

Parents were setting up playpens and putting sleepy babies in them. The coat hooks were filled, so people piled their wraps on the benches around the room.

At the south end of the room was a little stage for the band. Mrs. Madrid plays the upright piano, and Mr. Madrid plays fiddle. My dad plays guitar, and my mom sits behind her little drum set and beats out the rhythm. Dad's guitar case was lying open beside Mom's feet. I remember when my youngest sister, Julie, was a baby, and she slept in the guitar case. Mom says I slept there, too, when I was a baby.

Though the band had started to play, Julie was up on-stage saying something to Mom. Mom nodded her head in my direction, and Julie came running over. She begged me to dance with her. I was teaching her to do the dances I knew. Country-western dancing is not like square-dancing. There's no caller to tell you what to do; you have to know the steps yourself.

First Julie and I danced a polka. After that was over, the band played Ten Pretty Girls. Now, this dance is like the Cotton-Eyed Joe. It's got a lot of complicated moves in it. Julie pestered me to teach her, but I said, "You'll have to get someone else, Julie. I don't know it."

"Dad should be the one to teach me," Julie said. She was right. Usually mothers teach their sons, and fathers teach the daughters.

Just then Julie saw one of her friends and ran over to join her. I sat down on a bench. Across the room from me, I saw a stranger—a girl about my age sitting alone.

Most everyone at the dance wore Western shirts and jeans and cowboy boots. But this girl had on a long-sleeved dress that covered her knees. Her hair hung straight and blond. She looked like Alice in Wonderland.

I worked my way around the end of the room, staying out of the way of the dancing couples.

When I stood in front of her, she didn't look up at me until I spoke. "Hello," I said. "This is your first time here, isn't it?"

She looked at me with wide-open misty blue eyes. "Yes," she said. "I'm visiting my aunt and uncle. They brought me tonight because I love country-western dancing. My name's Alice."

That's easy to remember, I thought. "My name's Mark," I said. "They're starting to play a polka now. Would you like to dance?"

I held out my hand to her and waited until she put her hand up. I took hold of it and held it until she stood. Her blue eyes did not look into mine, but stared past my right ear. Then she did a strange thing. With her free hand, she felt my shoulder, then my neck, then touched the top of my head.

"So I know how tall you are," she said.

I dropped her hand as if it were a hot potato. "You're blind," I said. Then I knew how rude that was. But I'd never been around blind people. I didn't know how you're supposed to talk to them or treat them.

"I'm sorry," I said. "I didn't know. You probably don't want to dance. You might get hurt in this crowd."

"Don't be silly," she said. "I can dance very well. I just need a partner to guide me. Don't you want to?" Her voice sounded as if she were daring me.

"Sure." I put my arm around her waist very lightly and just barely touched her hand.

"For goodness sake, I'm not going to break. Take a good hold of me. I'm just like any other girl you might dance with," she said. "Blindness is a bother when I want to read or when I'm buying a dress, but it's no bother here."

I took her at her word. I figured she knew a lot more about being blind than I did. I swung her out into the middle of the room and found myself dancing better than I ever had before. The polka steps came out of my legs and feet as easy as the rhythm from my mom's drums.

"That was great," I said and held her hand to show her that I wanted her to be my partner for the next dance.

When the music started again, it was the Cotton-Eyed Joe. I was disappointed because now I had to let her go. Someone else would want to dance with her because she was so good. I led her to the bench where she had been sitting.

"Don't you want to dance this one?" Alice asked.

"I don't know how."

"I'll teach you." She pulled my arms until they were in the right place and our hands were held just so. "Now, watch my feet and listen." We joined the other couples circling the dance floor.

"Now put your left hand around my waist and your right out front," she whispered. She was a good teacher. I don't believe I ever learned anything so fast in my life.

When other boys saw how good she was, they started asking her to dance. Then the band played Ten Pretty Girls, and I got her to teach me that dance, too.

At midnight the band stopped playing, and we lined up at the table to fill our plates with food. I helped Alice get what she wanted on her plate.

While we ate, Alice told silly elephant jokes. I can't remember them, but she must have known a hundred. We laughed and had fun.

The next day I thought about what I had learned. Making a new friend is sort of like magic. Like Lake Valley on a Saturday night. You're in a dark place. Then the lights go on. And a ghost town comes alive with music and dancing.

ABOUT THE AUTHOR

JOANN MAZZIO

After graduating from university, Joann Mazzio worked as an aeronautical engineer. She then taught math for fifteen years in New Mexico before becoming a full-time writer. She has written two novels, including *Leaving Eldorado*, which is set in her hometown of Pinos Altos, New Mexico. She has also written a biography and several pieces of short fiction and non-fiction for magazines. Joann has two adult children, and also a turtle named Hattie.

All the Places to Love

by Patricia MacLachlan
Illustrated by Mike Wimmer

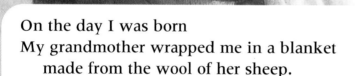

On the day I was born
My grandmother wrapped me in a blanket
    made from the wool of her sheep.

She held me up in the open window
So that what I heard first was the wind.
What I saw first were all the places to love:
The valley,
The river falling down over rocks,
The hilltop where the blueberries grew.

My grandfather was painting the barn,
And when he saw me he cried.
He carved my name—ELI—
On a rafter beside his name
And Grandmother's name
And the names of my papa and mama.

Mama carried me on her shoulders before I could walk,
Through the meadows and hay fields.
The cows watched us and the sheep scattered;
The dogs ran ahead, looking back with sly smiles.
When the grass was high
Only their tails showed.

When I was older, Papa and I plowed the fields.
Where else is soil so sweet? he said.
Once Papa and I lay down in the field, holding hands,
And the birds surrounded us:
Raucous black grackles, redwings,
Crows in the dirt that swaggered like pirates.
When we left, Papa put a handful of dirt in his pocket.
I did too.

My grandmother loved the river best of all the places to love.
That sound, like a whisper, she said;
Gathering in pools
Where trout flashed like jewels in the sunlight.
Grandmother sailed little bark boats downriver to me
With messages.
I Love You Eli, one said.

We jumped from rock to rock to rock,
Across the river to where the woods began,
Where bunchberry grew under the pine-needle path
And trillium bloomed.
Under the beech tree was a soft, rounded bed where a deer had slept.
The bed was warm when I touched it.

When spring rains came and the meadow turned to
   marsh,
Cattails stood like guards, and killdeers called.
Ducks nested by marsh marigolds,
And the old turtle—his shell all worn—
No matter how slow,
Still surprised me.

Sometimes we climbed to the place Mama loved best,
With our blueberry buckets and a chair for my
   grandmother:
To the blueberry barren where no trees grew—
The sky an arm's length away;
Where marsh hawks skimmed over the land,
And bears came to eat fruit,
And wild turkeys left footprints for us to find,
Like messages.
Where else, said my mama, *can I see the sun
   rise on one side
And the sun set on the other?*

My grandfather's barn is sweet-smelling and dark and cool;
Leather harnesses hang like paintings against old wood;
And hay dust floats like gold in the air.
Grandfather once lived in the city,
And once he lived by the sea;
But the barn is the place he loves most.
Where else, he says, *can the soft sound of cows chewing*
Make all the difference in the world?

Today we wait, him sitting on a wooden-slat chair
And me on the hay,
Until, much later, my grandmother holds up a small bundle
    in the open window,
Wrapped in a blanket made from the wool of her sheep,
And my grandfather cries.

Together
We carve the name SYLVIE in the rafter
Beside the names of Grandfather and Grandmother,
And my mama and papa,
And me.

My sister is born.

Someday I might live in the city.
Someday I might live by the sea.
But soon I will carry Sylvie on my
    shoulders through the fields;
I will send her messages downriver
    in small boats;
And I will watch her at the top of the hill,
Trying to touch the sky.
I will show her my favorite place, the marsh,
Where ducklings follow their mother
Like tiny tumbles of leaves.

All the places to love are here, I'll tell her,
    no matter where you may live.
Where else, I will say, *does an old turtle crossing the path*
Make all the difference in the world?

Speak Your Dreams

Poems by Langston Hughes
Illustrated by Stephen Taylor

The Dream Keeper

Bring me all of your dreams,
You dreamers,
Bring me all of your
Heart melodies
That I may wrap them
In a blue cloud-cloth
Away from the too-rough fingers
Of the world.

To You

To sit and dream, to sit and read,
To sit and learn about the world
Outside our world of here and now—
    Our problem world—
To dream of vast horizons of the soul
Through dreams made whole,
Unfettered, free—help me!
All you who are dreamers too,
    Help me to make
    Our world anew.
I reach out my dreams to you.

The Smile

As the day begins and the sun is shining bright,
The birds are singing and everything is going right.
A smile will do you good on this wonderful day,
As one girl did when she went out to play.
Her name is Sue, and at the break of dawn
As soon as she woke up she put a smile on.
At school the kids call her Smilin' Sue,
And you'll soon know why when the day is through.

Sue was walking down the street; there out on his lawn
Was her friend, so she smiled at Juan.
Juan was biking along with a happy face;
In a window was his friend, so he smiled at Grace.
When Grace went outside that bright sunny day
She smiled at Mira, who smiled at Faye.
Faye smiled at Connie, who smiled at Ran,
Who smiled at Zach, the ice-cream man.
Zach smiled at Nadia, who smiled at Kitty,
And soon not just the town was smiling
But the whole city!
Then the countries and even the world smiled that day.
In outer space the aliens too smiled
but in their own way.
Now do you see what started because of that one girl, Sue?
So keep on smiling is my message to you,
And you'll soon see what a smile can do.

Oh, my! I see that you're smiling too!

Taryn Green
Age 13

Taryn Green

> Writing is the creative act of freely expressing your imagination. I forge my thoughts onto paper in a symphony of words.

Tamzin El-Fityani

Sign Language

Gesturing may be used by people who are hard of hearing, people who speak different languages, or people who are involved in silent rituals. Sign language is a formal method of communication used by people who are hearing impaired. In the United States, American Sign Language (ASL) is the fourth most commonly used language. In 1760, in Paris, the Abbe Charles Michel de L'Epee founded the first public school for the deaf. The basis of instruction was the signs used by the hearing impaired in Paris. Sign language came to the United States when Laurent Clerc, a hearing-impaired graduate, was named the first head instructor of the American Institution for the Deaf and the Dumb. Most of the signs in ASL represent words or word groups and must be used in sentences according to a distinct grammar. Sign language is a proper language, and it helps the hearing impaired communicate without sound.

Tamzin El-Fityani
Grade 6

LIBRARY
Meridian Heights School